AF573597

Kittens

Rachael Hale brings you the world's most lovable animals. Friends for life. Unique characters and enchanting personalities beautifully captured to inspire and delight all ages.

Established in New Zealand in 1995, Rachael Hale is now a global success story, loved by millions around the world and regularly receiving international acclaim.

KITTENS

Designed and edited by WPL
Photography courtesy of RACHAEL HALE PHOTOGRAPHY LTD.

Printed in China
Published by WPL 2007

ISBN 978-1-904264-48-4

WPL
The Perfume Factory
140 Wales Farm Road
London W3 6UG
Tel: +44 (0) 208 993 7268
Fax: +44 (0) 208 993 8041
email: info@wpl.eu.com
www.wpl.eu.com

The smallest feline is a

masterpiece.

[LEONARDO DA VINCI]

To err is human, to

purr

is feline.

[AUTHOR UNKNOWN]

Anyone who says you can't buy happiness

has forgotten about

kittens.

[WILFRED P. LAMPTON]

An ordinary kitten will ask more

questions

than any five-year-old.

[CARL VAN VECHTEN]

There is no more intrepid

explorer than a kitten.

[JULES CHAMPFLEURY]

Nowhere is out of bounds

for a **kitten.**

Even a cat is a **lion** in her own lair.

[JULES CHAMPFLEURY]

If only cats grew into

kittens.

[R. STERN]

It is **impossible**

to keep a straight face in the

presence of one or more kittens.

[CYNTHIA E. VARNADO]

A kitten can **purr** its way out of anything.

[RUTH HANLON]

There is no 'snooze' button

on a **kitten**

who wants breakfast.

[ANON]

Prowling in his own quiet backyard
or asleep by the fire, a kitten is still only
a whisker away
from the **wilds.**

[JEAN BURDEN]

Kittens are **miracles**

with paws.

[ANON]

Kittens

are born with their eyes shut.
They open them in about six days,
take a look around, then close them again
for the better part of their lives.

[STEPHEN BAKER]

A kitten can sleep

anywhere at any time.

There is no such thing as a kitten with insomnia.

[JACQUELINE FRANCIS]

There can't be a **better** life than a kitten's - doing what they like, when they like, as much as they like.

[RICARDO PHILIPS]

Happiness

is a small, warm, ball of fur.

[FRANCIS WICKHAM]

Consciousness: that annoying time

between **naps.**

[ANON]

A cat has **nine** lives.

For three he plays,

for three he strays,

and for the last three he stays.

[ENGLISH PROVERB]

A **meow** massages the heart.

[STUART McMILLAN]

Our **perfect** companions

never have fewer than four feet.

[COLETTE]

I purr,

therefore I am.

[ANON]

The more people I meet
the more I like my **cat.**

[ANON]

It's easy to be smitten by a

kitten.